CHRISTIANS

can possess
Demons
but they

CANNOT
BE POSSESSED

by them

**An in-depth Bible study about the
presence and operation of DEMONS
in the life of the believer in CHRIST**

NORMAN PARISH

Christians can possess Demons but they *Cannot Be Possessed* by them, Norman Parish
ISBN # 0-89228-140-5
Copyright ©1999, Norman Parish

Impact Christian Books, Inc.
332 Leffingwell Ave., Suite 101,
Kirkwood, MO 63122
314-822-3309
Website: *www.impactchristianbooks.com*

Cover Design: Ideations

Printed in the United States of America

CONTENTS

DEDICATION

*I dedicate this book to my wife, **Betty**, who during 42 years of marriage has loved me and supported me unconditionally. Thanks **Betty**, for being a true "help meet." Without you, my ministry would have never had the impact it has had. Your service to God and His people has been greatly admired and appreciated by all.*

NORMAN

Unless otherwise stated, all Scripture quotations were taken from the authorized King James Version of the Bible. Brief quotations in this book from other versions of the Bible are identified by the following codes:

CONT = Contemporary English Bible
GNMM = Good News to Modern Man
MOF = The New Testament: A New Translation (Moffatt)
NASB = New American Standard Bible
NEB = New English Bible
NIV = New International Version
NKJV = New King James Version
NOR = The New Testament: A New Translation (Norlie)
PHIL = The New Testament in Modern English (Phillips)
RSV = Revised Standard Version
TCNT = The Twentieth Century New Testament
WEY = The New Testament in Modern Speech (Weymouth)
WMS = The New Testament: A Translation in the Language
of the People (Williams)

PROLOGUE

The Beginnings of Our Involvement In the Deliverance Ministry

In August of 1963 we were abruptly introduced to the Deliverance Ministry. A week-long pastors' retreat was being held at a small, rustic camp owned by the mission west of Guatemala City. The retreat had been convened to study the end-time outpouring of the Holy Spirit upon the church and the world. From the very first night, the presence of God's Spirit was quite intense—convicting, breaking, humbling God's servants and preparing them for the blessings He was about to bestow. During the next several days, the majority of the pastors and workers in attendance were filled with the Holy Spirit, in accordance with Acts 1:4-5,8 and 2:4.

On the third day of the retreat, we came face to face with our first case of demon possession. A group of five women (including the wife of a Presbyterian medical doctor) arrived uninvited at the campgrounds in the early morning hours, hoping to listen to some of the Bible studies that were being imparted that week. Halfway through one of the sessions, a 20-year-old girl (a new-born Christian and, as we discovered later, the daughter of a psychic healer and warlock) began to manifest demons violently. All of us "froze," because we had never seen such a shocking display of demonic power.

The sister who at the moment was sharing from the Word, a missionary in Mexico, Margaret Erdman (editor of the Spanish issue of *The Herald of His Coming*), was the only person present who had had any experience (though rather limited) in dealing with such cases. Naturally, the Bible study was interrupted to give way to a period of intense spiritual warfare which ultimately lasted 72 hours non-stop. By Saturday morning the girl had been delivered of over 450 demons. To our amazement, several pastors also began to manifest symptoms of a strong demonic oppression in their lives and, as a consequence, had to be ministered to immediately. Being of a conservative background, all of this took us by surprise, to say the least.

During my three years of theological and ministerial studies in a solid fundamental Bible College on the West Coast of the United States, I never received a single course on demonology. This topic—as well as many others, such as the baptism in the Holy Spirit, healing, miracles, tongues, visions and so forth—was considered taboo. I remember that during those formative years a couple of books passed through my hands, which I read more out of curiosity than with a sincere desire to learn: *Demon Possession*, written by a missionary in China whose surname was Nevius, and *War on the Saints*, a classic on spiritual warfare written by Jessie Penn-Lewis. That was the limit of my preparation for confronting the barrage of deliverance cases that would soon overwhelm us.

At the conclusion of the pastors' retreat, the meetings were transferred to our mother church in Guatemala City. There also, the Holy Spirit was manifested in a mighty way. The testimony of the demonized girl caused quite a commotion. During the Sunday morning altar call, several young men and women (including the president of the young people's society) manifested demons, since they had been involved (without our even suspecting it) in witchcraft, sexual immorality or drugs. That evening, many persons were anointed with the Holy Spirit and equipped with spiritual gifts for the edification of the Body of Christ. This was truly the beginning of the Deliverance Ministry in Guatemala and perhaps in all of Central America.

In the following months hundreds of people from all over the country came seeking deliverance and healing. The majority were members and leaders of churches of many different missions and denominations. When they returned to their congregations, euphorically testifying to their deliverance from demons and diseases, a wave of rejection and persecution arose against us on the part of the pastors who weren't personally acquainted with this ministry. We were even accused of practicing a refined type of spiritualism, because the demons sometimes manifested assuming the names of dead persons, including many Catholic saints.

Due to our lack of experience, this open conflict with the forces of evil became exhausting, since we spent long hours (even entire nights) combating and expelling demons. As time went by, God gave us wisdom to properly take care of this onslaught of people who were seriously affected (physically, mentally, emotionally, morally and spiritually) by demons and curses, without wearing ourselves out completely in the process. Thousands of men and women contaminated by evil spirits filed through the doors of that church—and most of them professed to be born-again Christians, even pastors and leaders of evangelical and Pentecostal churches! Though the battle was (and still is!) intense—and as a result we have suffered the counter-attacks of the enemy—we never lost heart or gave up, as some unfortunately have.

The Deliverance Ministry spread slowly from Guatemala to other countries on the American continent. Many churches and missions that previously rejected and openly opposed it are now involved in it, to one degree or another for the benefit of God's people. Through the years we have been invited to hold seminars on deliverance and spiritual warfare in many nations. The results have been truly amazing. Thousands of sincere believers have shown their desperate need for deliverance and their keen interest in learning how they can be used of God to deliver others.

I trust that as you read this book, you also will be encouraged to experience "the glorious liberty of the children of God" (Romans 8:21) that only Jesus Christ can offer (John 8:36; Galatians 5: 1). Only then will you be qualified to minister to others that suffer and groan under Satan's bondage.

Introduction

When we propose to study certain biblical doctrines, we soon discover that there usually is a crucial point that tends to divide Christians into two hostile camps. What seems strange, especially to believers that have little theological expertise, is that the opponents find texts in the Bible that support "beyond question" their conflicting points of view. The partisans of these extreme positions tend to establish a premise and then go to the Word of God to find verses that seem to support it.

For example, in relation to the doctrine of salvation there are many ministers that proclaim vehemently that salvation is "only by grace through faith in Jesus Christ," while others teach tenaciously and dogmatically that salvation is by faith plus meritorious works, such as: the observance of certain mosaic laws, the keeping of the Sabbath, water baptism (according to some particular formula), the holy sacraments, acts of benevolence, tithing, etc.

Certain theologians affirm that salvation cannot be lost under any circumstance (the Calvinists: "once saved, always saved"), while others allow that salvation can be lost when the believer consciously and deliberately turns his back on God and with full use of his mental capabilities goes back to sinning and indulging in worldly pleasures (the Arminians).

In reference to the doctrine of the Holy Spirit, some teach that after salvation you must have another experience in God called the baptism in or with the Holy Spirit, that is evidenced by the supernatural ability of "speaking in other tongues" (Acts 10:44-46; 2:4; 19:6). All Pentecostals and most Charismatics affirm this. On the contrary, there are others, mostly conservative evangelicals, that proclaim that when a person is converted at the same moment he receives all that God offers in Christ and that there is no need to seek or ask for an additional spiritual experience that will enable him to live a victorious Christian life.

There are many respectable Christians that firmly believe that today we can have the gifts of the Holy Spirit (as described in 1 Corinthians chapters 12 and 14) in full operation in our lives and churches, since those gifts were given by Jesus Christ for the edification of His Church during the entire Age of Grace (1 Corinthians 1:5-8). In contrast, there are other Christians, equally worthy of our respect, that avow that the operation of the gifts of the Spirit ceased when the apostolic era drew to a close or when the sacred canon (the Bible) was completed towards the end of the 4th century (1 Corinthians 13:9-10).

In like manner, when we consider the Deliverance Ministry, we discover that due to the fact that it has become such a controversial subject, it tends to polarize and, regrettably, divide the Body of Christ. The debate centers around the question of whether a believer, regenerated and indwelt by the Holy Spirit, can "have" demons. Many churches—both denominational and independent, fundamentalist and even Pentecostal—have taken extreme positions, some adamantly against the idea that born-again believers can "have" demons and others decidedly in favor.

A great majority of our conservative theologians affirm categorically that a true believer, being the temple of God, cannot "have" demons, because it is impossible for the Holy Spirit to cohabit the same body with unclean spirits. Others, that constitute a respectable minority, assert that **Christians can possess demons, but that they cannot be possessed by them.**

Those who teach that a believer in Christ cannot "have" demons, maintain that all demons leave at the exact moment the person receives Christ in his heart. Would to God that were true, because at conversion all problems caused by the presence of evil spirits in man's inner being (such as oppressions, phobias, addictions, illnesses, etc.) would be instantly cured. Nevertheless, experience teaches us that many believers, even after their personal encounter with Christ, continue to face serious physical, moral, emotional, mental and spiritual problems that have no human explanation or solution. Only by experiencing the fullness of Christ's redemptive work on the cross, applied to us by the Holy Spirit in answer to active faith, can the redeemed be liberated and restored, and this usually in a gradual or progressive way.

In order to determine if demons can or cannot dwell and operate in the life of a believer you must go directly to the Word of God. Our experience, no matter how vast or relevant it might seem, cannot serve as the basis on which to establish a doctrinal belief, especially when we approach a subject that is so sensitive and intricate as this one. The Word says in Isaiah 8:20: "To the law and to the testimony: if they speak not according to this word, it is because there is no light in them." Paul also affirms in 1 Corinthians 4:6: "...that ye might learn in us not to think... above that which is written..." In reference to this verse, another little-known version suggests that we ought "not go beyond what the Scriptures permit" (NOR). Therefore, we must limit ourselves to the teachings of the Holy Scriptures, without twisting them or taking them out of context, so that in the end we can decide if in truth the believer today can be infested or not in certain areas of his personal life by unclean spirits.

When you demand scriptural proof of those who oppose the idea that a believer can "have" demons, they can scarcely produce any and even the few they present are not as convincing or conclusive as they ought to be. Some 30 years ago or more, while reading an issue of a popular magazine called *Christian Life*, I discovered a column of questions and answers written by Dr. Edman, president at the time of Wheaton College, a prestigious Christian institution of higher learning. A reader of the magazine had sent in to ask if a born-again believer could "have" demons, to which the writer answered more or less in these terms: On the basis of experience—yes! On the basis of Scripture—no!

The writer related that during the years when he had

served as an evangelical missionary in Ecuador, he had known of several cases of demonic influence, or possession, in persons that claimed to be Christians. Most assuredly, to him as a representative of one the most conservative branches of the evangelical church, it had been rather perplexing to have known of cases where demons had to be cast out of persons that were obviously members of the Body of Christ, since that was in open contradiction to the beliefs that are tenaciously held by the majority of Christian leaders—that it is impossible for a true believer to "have" demons.

When I read this article I determined to study the Scriptures in depth to see if I could come up with the biblical evidence needed to prove that a Christian could be affected in his innermost being by evil spirits. I already had ample experience in dealing with cases of believers that were demonized and even bewitched, but I needed solid scriptural proof on which to build a ministry that is absolutely essential in the end-times—the Deliverance Ministry.

During several months I dedicated myself to studying the subject conscientiously, both in the Old and New Testaments, with the idea of discarding deliverance completely in the event I couldn't prove by the Scriptures that a Christian could be invaded or infected by demons. At the end of this period of intensive study I arrived at the conclusion that the Bible does teach that a believer can "have" demons. In this book—written mainly for the benefit of average Christians and not so much for scholars—I present the cases and texts taken directly from the Bible that, **studied as a whole,** prove conclusively (in my opinion) that even a true believer can be oppressed from the inside by evil spirits.

As we prepare to study certain specific Bible passages that reveal that a follower of Christ can be infested, contaminated, plagued or harassed by demonic spirits, we must first define at least two words that are commonly used in circles where deliverance is practiced seriously, and these words are: deliverance and demonized.

The word "deliverance" is a derivative of the verb "deliver" that according to the dictionary means, among other things, "to loose, untie, unbind, release, let go, liberate, set free, emancipate and redeem." Deliverance, therefore, is the act—instantaneous or progressive—of loosing, liberating, emancipating, etc. Applying this to our Christian life and experience, deliverance is the act or process by which a human being is liberated from the oppression or captivity of Satan through the power of the Holy Spirit (Matthew 12:28).

When Christ ministered on a certain Sabbath day to a woman that was bent over (Luke 13:10-17), He refuted the critical remarks of His most vicious opponents by stating that Satan had bound her during eighteen years and that, consequently, it was necessary to loose her of this "bond," identifying the cause of her pitiful condition. The colt Jesus was going to ride in His triumphant entry into Jerusalem was tied to a post in the outskirts of the city (Luke 19:28-38) and had to be "loosed" before Jesus could use it as His means of transportation. Lazarus, when brought back to life, was "bound hand and foot," which forced Jesus to issue an order: "Loose him, and let him go" (John 11:44). In the same manner, many people who receive eternal life in Christ Jesus today are "bound" by ancestral curses, psychic powers, chronic diseases, base passions, mental disorders, destructive habits, etc., mostly satanic in nature, and thereby need to be liberated before God can effectually use them.

It is important not to confuse deliverance with "exorcism," a spiritualistic practice that sorcerers, psychic healers and other persons deeply involved in the occult use in a vain attempt to expel demons (Matthew 12:26). Through the use of entreaties, incantations, conjurations, charms, crystals, ritual cleansings, the burning of incense, sleight of hand, etc., the exorcists can only "appease" or "transfer" demons, but never expel them. The demons are merely relocated to another part of the body or to another member of the family, where they can freely continue their devastating work. The rite of exorcism has also been adopted by the Roman Catholic Church and by certain nominal Protestant churches which through the use of memorized prayers, rituals, crucifixes, holy water, etc., try to subjugate and dislodge the evil spirits that torment some of their parishioners.

The other word that needs to be defined is "demonized," which according to most dictionaries means: the state of being controlled or mastered by an evil spirit or influence. In the Scriptures "demonized" simply refers to a person that "has demons" or is a demoniac. The use of the word "possessed" by the King James Version and several modern translations (such as the RSV, NEB, NIV, PHIL, etc.) is most unfortunate. A much better word would have been "demonized." The verb possess means to own and control, to fill or take up entirely, to have full power and mastery over, to have and to hold, etc. Therefore, "possession" signifies the state of being owned and mastered by somebody, in this instance by an evil influence, which is impossible in the case of a born-again Christian, for he was bought (redeemed) at a great price and therefore belongs to God (1 Corinthians 6:20; 7:23; 1 Peter 1:18-19).

The King James Version says that the Gadarean "was possessed of devils" because he "had devils long time" (Luke 8:36,27), but a much better translation would be "was demonized." Christ's enemies accused him several times of "having" demons (John 7:20; 8:48,52; 10:20,21) or of being a demoniac, which actually means the same thing. In conclusion, to be "demonized" simply means to "have" demons, without determining the degree of influence or possession that they have obtained. It is advisable not to use the word "possessed" when referring to a brother or sister in Christ who might be under the influence of demons, because it is widely believed that to be "possessed" means that the person is a lunatic or a maniac and, therefore, is fully insane.

Although I am not a "bibliolater," after reading and studying the Bible for over 45 years (both in the English and Spanish) I still prefer the King James Version, for I consider it to be the most faithful to the original

16

manuscripts. The translators of this version were not influenced by higher criticism or by some of the modern theological trends, such as liberalism or neo-orthodoxy, that are many times prone to dilute the true meaning of the Scriptures. Nevertheless, we must rightfully acknowledge that some recent versions help clarify certain biblical concepts that are hard to understand in the King James due to the subtle changes that have taken place over the years in the meaning of many words of the English language. When necessary or beneficial, I will quote from some of these newer translations.

I strongly recommend that before you read and study the rest of this book, you stop for a moment to ask the Lord to liberate you from any preconceived notions and doctrinal prejudices that were implanted in your mind and heart by the churches and seminaries you have attended. Try to approach the subject dealt with in this book with a open mind, that is with a mind that has been liberated and renewed by the Holy Spirit (1 Corinthians 2:14-16).

Please remember that the things of the Spirit must be "spiritually discerned" under the direct guidance and illumination of the Holy Spirit. It is of utmost importance that during this study you use the Holy Scriptures extensively, reading carefully each biblical reference, in order to make sure that the Holy Spirit leads you into all truth (John 16:13). If you have several versions of the Bible, consult them freely, because they can cast light on some of the passages that might be obscure, and thus hard to understand or interpret due to the delicate nature of the topic we are studying.

SECTION I

How Demons Operate
In the Life of the Believer

In order to understand the operation of demons in the life of the believer, it is necessary to study the subject of Body, Soul and Spirit. While modern Psychology —which denies the existence of the spirit (whether it be human, divine or demonic)—teaches the dichotomy of man (that he is only mind and body), the Bible teaches that man is a trichotomy. In 1 Thessalonians 5:23, Paul says:

And the very God of peace sanctify you wholly; and I pray God your whole spirit and soul and body be preserved blameless unto the coming of our Lord Jesus Christ.

It is obvious that this biblical passage teaches that

man is a triune, or tripartite being, consisting of spirit, soul and body. Also, in Hebrews 4:12 it says:

> *For the Word of God is quick, and powerful, and sharper than any two-edged sword, piercing even to the dividing asunder of soul and spirit, and of the joints and marrow, and is a discerner of the thoughts and intents of the heart.*

When we examine this portion of Scripture, we discover that the author of the epistle speaks of soul and spirit, but also of "the joints and marrow" (body) and of "the thoughts and intents of the heart" (mind). According to renown expositors of the Bible, the soul is also a trilogy, consisting of mind (thoughts), will (decisions) and heart (emotions). In conclusion, we can affirm that man is a spirit (Job 34:14; Proverbs 18:14; 20:27; Ecclesiastes 3:21; 8:8; 12:7; Zechariah 12:1; 1 Corinthians 2:11), that he has a soul and lives in a body with which he relates to the environment that surrounds him.

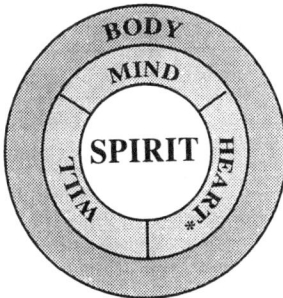

*Feelings, emotions and personal affections.

In the natural man (the unconverted), the spirit is "dead," as Paul teaches in Ephesians 2:1,5 ("And you hath he quickened, who were dead in trespasses and sins"), in Colossians 2:13 ("And you, being dead in your sins ... hath he quickened together with him...") and in 1 Timothy 5:6 ("But she that liveth in pleasure is dead (spiritually) while she liveth (physically)." Due to this fact, man without the knowledge of God is virtually a dual being (body and soul), since his spirit is "dead," that is, in a state of abeyance or latency and, as such, inert (inactive or inoperative).

Spiritual death, according to theologians, is "separation from God." Due to sin, an insurmountable barrier was raised between God and man (Isaiah 59:2), that only Jesus Christ by His atoning death on the cross can tear down (Romans 5:10; Ephesians 2:13,16-18). To believe intuitively or intellectually in the existence of a Supreme Being, as many religious and non-religious people do today, doesn't insure that man will have a consciousness or awareness of God, or maintain a relationship with Him. That is only possible through the Lord Jesus Christ (John 14:6).

THE NATURAL MAN

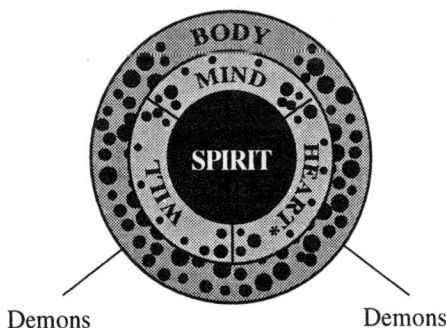

Demons   Demons

21

The initial work of the Holy Spirit in man, when he finally listens and heeds the message of salvation in Jesus Christ, is to reprove man (John 16:8; Acts 2:37) and awaken or sensitize his conscience so that he can feel the guilt of his sin (2 Corinthians 7:9-10), repent and by faith receive Jesus Christ as His Sin-bearer and Savior. At that moment, a real miracle takes place in him, the greatest miracle of all—the new birth (John 3:3,5). God creates in him, in his spirit, "the new creation" (2 Corinthians 5:17). "The new man, which after God is created in righteousness and true holiness" (Ephesians 4:24) is a holy creature that "doth not commit sin" (1 John 3:9; 5:18) or, as other versions reword it, "cannot keep on sinning" (CONT) or "cannot practice sinning" (WMS).

From the moment that man receives Jesus Christ as his Savior, the Holy Spirit comes to dwell or reside in him (Romans 8:9). Consequently, man becomes "an habitation of God through the Spirit" (Ephesians 2:22). In the Spanish equivalent to the King James Version this verse is translated: "a dwelling-place for God in the (human) spirit." Combining what is said in these two versions, we can affirm that redeemed man is the habitation of God in the spirit (human) and by the Spirit (divine).

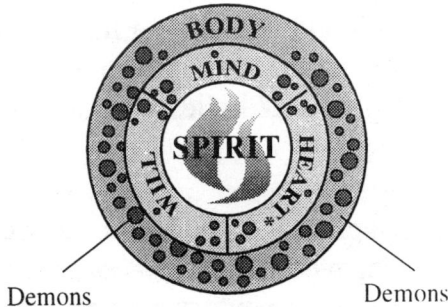

Paul also calls the believer in Christ "the temple of God" in 1 Corinthians 3:16-17 and 6:19:

Know ye not that ye are the temple of God, and that the Spirit of God dwelleth in you? If any man defile (desecrate, destroy) the temple of God, him shall God destroy; for the temple of God is holy, which temple ye are.

What? Know ye not that your body is the temple of the Holy Ghost which is in you, which ye have of God, and ye are not your own?

Both the tabernacle erected by Moses in the wilderness and the temple built by Solomon in Jerusalem had three main areas: (1) the outer court; (2) the holy place; and (3) the holy of holies. According to Bible typology, the outer court represents the believer's body; the holy place, his soul; and the holy of holies, his spirit.

23

All had access to the outer court, including the Gentiles; to the holy place, the ministers (priests and Levites); but to the holy of holies, only the High Priest, once a year, and not without blood to atone for his own sins and for the sins of his people. Any unauthorized person that dared enter the holy of holies was smitten by God's power.

Making a spiritual application to the preceding passages, we discover that demons can invade the body and soul of the believer, when the circumstances allow them to, but can never penetrate his "holy of holies" (the regenerated spirit) which has been reserved exclusively for the "High Priest of our profession, Christ Jesus" (Hebrews 3:1). Although I have ministered to thousands of Christians with serious demonic problems in their bodies and souls, I have never found one that had demons in his spirit. That can only mean that **Christians can be infested, bound, oppressed, captivated, obsessed, etc., by demons, but never possessed.**

THE TWO NATURES OF THE BELIEVER

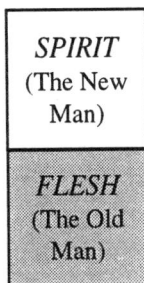

SPIRIT (The New Man)
FLESH (The Old Man)

In the regenerated man exist two natures: the human (called "the old man" or flesh) and the divine (called the "new man" or spirit). In relation to this subject, I would strongly advise you to stop right now and read Ephesians 4:22-24, Colossians 3:9-11 and Romans 6:4,6. The "old man," our sinful and depraved human nature, inhabits the body and the soul of the believer; on the other hand, the "new man," as a holy and perfect divine nature, inhabits the spirit.

The flesh (the "old man") and the spirit (the "new man") continuously oppose each other. For that reason, in the soul of most believers there is a constant, raging battle, that Paul describes in Romans 7:14-25 and in Galatians 5:16-17. That conflict is in great part aroused and inflamed by the unclean spirits that operate in the "old man" of the believer. The demons reinforce and excite the flesh so that it may resist the Holy Spirit that dwells and operates in the regenerated spirit of man.

THE BATTLE FIELD

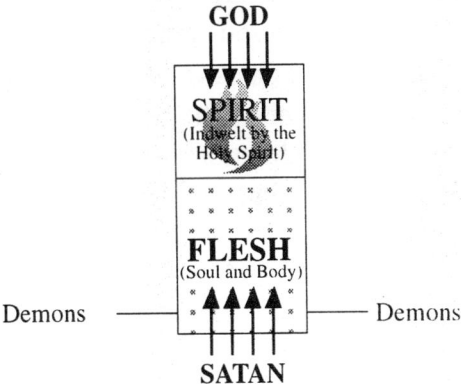

GOD

SPIRIT
(Indwelt by the
Holy Spirit)

FLESH
(Soul and Body)

Demons ——— | ——— Demons

SATAN

25

If the Holy Spirit is willing to inhabit the same body with the "old man" (that is truly a satanic creature, worse than any demon!), should it be difficult for us to believe that He is willing to dwell momentarily in a body that is contaminated by evil spirits? Scripture reveals that the flesh "is not subject to the law of God, neither indeed can be" (Romans 8:7). Demons, on the other hand, can be subjected in the name of Jesus (Luke 10:17). The flesh, as the unredeemed human nature, cannot be cast out; demons can be cast out, when the person admits that he has them and is willing to submit to God in order to be set free.

There is only one remedy for the flesh that resides in us: crucifixion, which is a constant and conscious identification with the death of Christ (Romans 6:6,11). Another is the remedy for the evil spirits that operate in our being: liberation. The flesh must be mortified (Romans 8:13; Colossians 3:5) or crucified (Galatians 5:24), but, demons must be bound and expelled by the anointing of the Holy Spirit (Matthew 12:28; Luke 4:18; Acts 10:38; Isaiah 10:27). Regrettably, you cannot "cast out" the flesh; neither can you "crucify" the demons. The solution is different in each case. Once the demons have been cast out, the believer by the Spirit can begin to take dominion over his flesh, mortifying it, restraining it, subjecting it to the obedience of Jesus Christ.

SECTION II

Clinical Cases:
Bible Characters That Were
Contaminated with Demons

I now present several specific examples of persons in the New Testament that had problems of a demonic origin. Some of these cases are obvious; others, not quite so obvious. Although in the Old Testament there are some interesting and forceful cases of persons that were anointed as God's servants but were later taken and used by evil spirits (for example: Saul, the king, and Balaam, the prophet), I have deliberately omitted them in this study, because certain opponents of the Deliverance Ministry will claim that they are not valid since they lived before the Dispensation of Grace and, therefore, are not relevant to us in this present day and age.

CASE #1

JAMES AND JOHN

"Ye know not what manner of spirit ye are of"
—Luke 9:51-56—

According to this Bible story, the time when Jesus "should be received up" was drawing near. His crucifixion, resurrection and ascension were going to take place shortly. Knowing this, the Lord Jesus "steadfastly set his face to go to Jerusalem," for it was impossible "that a prophet should perish out of Jerusalem" (Luke 13:33). The trip from beyond the Jordan river (John 10:40) was slow and wearisome. Wherever He went, multitudes surrounded and besieged Him, because they longed to see some of His miracles, or to hear some of His teachings. The people that followed Him, out of necessity or curiosity, made it impossible for Him to advance as fast as He wanted to.

On His way through the province of Samaria, He discovered that as night came He was still in a place that was virtually uninhabited. Not cherishing the idea of sleeping in the outdoors, He sent several of His disciples ahead, to a nearby city populated entirely by Samaritans, to prepare lodging for Himself and His entourage.

The Samaritans, influenced doubtlessly by their deep antagonism towards the Jews due to the ill-treatment they had endured at their hands for several centuries, refused to receive Him, especially knowing that His plan was to go up to Jerusalem to take part in the religious feast close at hand. The messengers returned crestfallen to the place where Jesus was waiting for them. When the rest of the disciples found out how they had been snubbed, they were outraged. James and John, the famous "sons of thunder," requested permission to cause fire to fall from heaven to consume all those renegade Samaritans.

Jesus rebuked them soundly, saying: "Ye know not what manner of spirit ye are of," insinuating that these disciples ignored what spirit was actually manifesting in and through them at that moment. Several versions (such as the RSV, NEB, NIV, etc.) eliminate this phrase entirely, perhaps because (among other reasons) some of their translators didn't believe that a follower of Christ could "have" demons.

It was obvious that James and John were being animated by another spirit and not by the Spirit of God. The words they spoke evidence attitudes that are contrary to the spirit of Christ, their Teacher and Master. James and John manifested a racist spirit—of intolerance, bigotry, prejudice, spite and even hatred towards the Samaritans. Apparently, it wouldn't matter to them if hundreds of innocent victims died, as long as they could take revenge for the offense received.

Jesus Christ had to remind them that He had come not "to destroy men's lives, but to save them." In the course of time, John experienced a deep transformation, becoming the "apostle of love." The Holy Spirit renewed his mind and cleansed his heart of these negative feelings and attitudes that he had developed due to family, racial and environmental influences.

This Bible passage compels us to admit the possibility that even Christ's closest associates could be influenced or motivated by a spirit foreign to the Spirit of God. It is necessary for us also to confess that at times we have felt anger, resentment, hatred, a sense of outrage, etc., when we have been abused, belittled or rejected. On more than one occasion, we too have felt constrained to get even or to take revenge. Such an attitude reveals that a spirit not of God is in control of some area of our life, seriously affecting our relationship with others (believers and non-believers) and hurting our testimony before the world.

CASE #2

SIMON PETER

"Get thee behind me, Satan"
—Matthew 16:21-23—

The time had come when it was necessary for the Lord Jesus to prepare His disciples for the tragic events that were about to take place in fulfillment of the divine and eternal plan, for Him and for all of humanity. Consequently, Christ began to reveal that it was imperative that He go up to Jerusalem to suffer, die and rise again on the third day. Peter, bold and indiscreet as usual, took Him aside and began to rebuke Him, saying, according to one creditable Spanish translation: "Have compassion on yourself; don't ever permit this to happen to you," trying thus to arouse His self-pity. Peter sought to activate in Christ the instinct of self-preservation, so that by all means He would avoid having to go to the cross to give His life in propitiation for the sins of all mankind.

Jesus immediately discerned that a spirit operated in Peter which opposed the realization of God's purposes for the human race. Without any hesitation or forbearance, He turned to Peter and said: "Get thee behind me, Satan: thou art an offence unto me." The word "offence" in the King James Version can be translated: hindrance, stumbling-block or snare. Another version translates this reprimand: "Get out of my way, you Satan, you are a hindrance to me" (TCNT). Evidently, Satan had access to Peter's mind and mouth and at that very moment was using him to dissuade or detain Jesus in the fulfillment of the plan of redemption.

Why could Satan take and use Peter so easily so that he might become unconsciously his instrument in trying to prevent Christ from fulfilling His divine mission? Let us remember that hours or days before Peter had been used by the Holy Spirit to make known one of the most transcendental revelations of the Holy Scriptures: the divinity of Christ (Matthew 16:13-19). Could it be possible that Peter misinterpreted the words of Christ (as so many have down through the centuries): "Thou art Peter, and upon this rock I will build my church...", and that as a result he began to think himself superior to the rest of the disciples? If this is true, it is not strange that pride or arrogance would have opened the doors to a demonic manifestation in his heart and life.

In a similar way, many of us have been attacked by the enemy, who with his customary cunningness has sought many times to awaken self-pity within us, causing us to think that no one really loves or understands us. We feel lonely and get depressed, and end up being easy prey to his "wiles" (schemes). This could even provoke in us certain emotional or mental disturbances that could have fatal consequences, including insanity and suicide.

"Satan hath desired to have you, that he may sift you as wheat"
—Luke 22:31—

The night that He was betrayed, Jesus Christ, after having celebrated the Passover with His disciples, made them a serious and solemn warning, that all of them would be scandalized and scattered (Matthew 26:31-33). Peter, trusting in himself, replied: "Though all men shall be offended because of thee, yet will I never be offended." With these words he reveals a certain type of pride and self-sufficiency, for it is quite evident that he believed he was stronger and braver than the rest of the disciples. His intentions were praiseworthy, but Peter's problem (common to all men) is that he didn't know himself well. "I am ready to go with thee, both into prison, and to death" (Luke 22:33), he insisted on saying, "I will lay down my life for thy sake" (John 13:37). He was sure that he would never deny or betray his Lord. And yet, Christ warned him that the same night he was going to be subjected to a terrible test, and that before sunrise he would deny Him three times.

Jesus knew by divine revelation that Satan had appeared before God's throne to ask permission to "sift" Peter as wheat (Luke 22:31,32). The sieve was an instrument used in agriculture to separate the wheat from the chaff and from other waste materials, in order to leave the grain clean enough to be taken to the mill to be converted into flour. Peter, as well as the rest of the disciples, was going to come under a heavy oppression of the enemy. "The power of darkness" (Luke 22:53) was going to rule supreme for several hours. God was going to allow Satan to treat Peter in an astute and cruel manner. This process was necessary to separate the "chaff" (flesh) from the "wheat" (spirit).

According to Matthew 26 and Luke 22, Peter, under the influence of Satan and his evil spirits, did several things that night which he would have never done if he had been in full control of his spiritual and mental abilities:

1) He fell into a deep sleep, together with John and James, members of Christ's inner circle (Matthew 26:36-45; Luke 22:39-46). The Lord reproached him for not being able to watch in prayer for one meager hour. It was on this occasion when He quoted those memorable words: "Watch and pray, that ye enter not into temptation" (Matthew 26:41).

2) He used the sword, supposedly to defend His Master (Matthew 26:51; Luke 22:50). One lesson he had never learned is that in spiritual warfare carnal weapons are totally useless (2 Corinthians 10:4-6).

3) He followed Jesus "afar off," not willing to identify fully with Him. In the process, he befriended the servants of the High Priest who was subjecting Christ to trial (Matthew 26:58; Luke 22:54).

4) He denied His Lord three consecutive times, cursing and swearing that he knew Him not (Matthew 26:69-74; Luke 22:55-60).

The Catholic Church avows today that the apostle Peter was the first Pope. Although evangelical Christians reject such an assertion (because of the lack of compelling or convincing historical and biblical evidence), it is necessary to recognize that Peter was God's chosen instrument to serve as leader of the Church in its first stage, described at length in the book of Acts chapters one through twelve. As such, he played an important role in introducing the Gospel in its fullness to the Jews (Acts 2), the Samaritans (Acts 8) and the Gentiles (Acts 10). Nevertheless, Peter was susceptible to demons, allowing himself to be used on more than one occasion by Satan in an attempt to hinder or delay God's plans.

CASE #3

JUDAS ISCARIOT

**"Have not I chosen you twelve, and one of
you is a devil"
—John 6:70—**

Jesus Christ was facing one of the first crises in His ministry. Many disciples, upon hearing His teaching about the cost and commitment of following Him, were offended and decided to turn back. Christ then asked the twelve, if they also wanted to desert Him. With deep conviction, Peter stepped forward to say: "Lord, to whom shall we go? thou (only) hast the words of eternal life."

It was at that moment Jesus insinuated that Satan had infiltrated the apostolic band. His words, "and one of you is a devil," could be better translated, "and one of you is the devil himself." Why was Satan able to seduce and later possess Judas so easily? Because he was a "thief" (John 12:6). Motivated by greed (Proverbs 1:19), he had probably been dishonest in handling the funds of the apostolic band.

Knowing who Judas was, Jesus nonetheless chose him from among the multitude of His disciples to be one of His twelve apostles (Mark 3:13-19). This was necessary "that the scripture might be fulfilled" (John 17:12). According to Mark 6:7,12-13, Jesus had endued him, as well as the rest of His apostles, with authority to

36

heal diseases and expel demons, and had sent them out to proclaim and demonstrate the Kingdom of God. Apparently, Judas had done so with compelling results.

When Christ's earthly ministry was coming to an end, the Scriptures say that Satan sowed into Judas' heart the idea of betraying Christ:

"...the devil having now put into the heart of Judas ... to betray him"
—John 13:2—

This passage proves that the devil had immediate access to Judas' heart (the seat of his affections and emotions). It is obvious that he had a blind ambition for power. In his sick mind, he had surmised many times that being, as he was, the treasurer of the apostolic band (John 12:6; 13:29), he would also become the "Secretary of the Treasury" in the kingdom that Jesus was going to establish. Disappointed because Jesus had not taken advantage of the opportunities afforded Him to become the King of the Jews (John 6:15), Judas decided that it would be best to betray and sell Him to His enemies, the religious leaders of Israel. Judas lent himself twice so that Satan himself (in person and not by means of some insignificant demon) could enter him and use him to carry out this nefarious deed. On the first occasion (Luke 22:3-6), when he was about to make the necessary arrangements to turn Jesus over to those that sought to kill Him, it declares that:

"Then entered Satan into Judas ..."

On the second (John 13:21-27), while he was still in the Upper Room with Jesus and His disciples, waiting for the right moment to gather and lead the mob that seized Jesus in the Garden of Gethsemane, it says that:

"...after the sop Satan entered into him"

It is entirely possible that by then Judas acted more like an automaton (or zombie), totally oblivious of what he was doing. His human personality was submerged, while at the same time Satan spoke and acted freely in and through him. Hours later, Judas had a rude awakening. When he came to himself, he realized that he had betrayed "innocent blood." Feeling great remorse, he made a vain attempt to cancel the deal (Matthew 27:3-5), but not achieving his purpose, he decided to take his own life.

Jesus Christ called Judas "the son of perdition" (John 17:12). Another influential personage, that will appear on the world stage in the end times, is similarly identified (2 Thessalonians 2:3). Some have affirmed that Judas will rise from the dead to fulfill this role in the years preceding the Second Coming of Christ. Whether this is true or not, we can be sure that in the likeness of Judas, this notable public figure (that some call the Antichrist) will be the incarnation of Satan himself.

If the four most prominent members of the apostolic band—Peter, James and John (His inner circle) and Judas

(His treasurer)—had bona fide demonic problems, how dare we affirm that we don't have them? We should at least explore that possibility and submit, if necessary, to a deliverance prayer to be free from them. The apostles evidently did, for in Matthew 10:8 Jesus says: "Heal the sick ... cast out devils: freely ye have received, freely give." It is clear that He was sending them to minister the things they had already received or experienced, deliverance being one of them.

CASE #4

THE WOMAN WITH THE SPIRIT OF INFIRMITY

"And, behold, there was a woman which had a spirit of infirmity eighteen years, and was bowed together..
—Luke 13:11—

Jesus Christ, as was His custom, was teaching or ministering in a synagogue on a certain Sabbath, when He noticed the presence of a poor woman that suffered from a degenerative disease in the congregation. Her body was bent over nearly to the ground, in such a way that she couldn't straighten up. She suffered from a curvature of the spine, caused perhaps by what doctors call "osteoporosis," a sickness common today in women over forty, brought about by the decalcification of the bones. This physical ailment hindered her from fulfilling the simplest household chores.

Moved by compassion, Jesus called her and set her free, saying: "Woman, thou art loosed from thine infirmity." On this occasion, He didn't rebuke or bind the demon, but He used an uncommon method in deliverance: using His spiritual authority, he declared her free from that terrible bondage. Although she was free from the evil spirit that crippled her, the woman was still stooped. Following that, He drew closer and laid hands on her, as He frequently did when ministering to the sick (Luke 4:40). Immediately the woman straightened up and began to glorify God for the double miracle she had received, first deliverance and then healing. If anyone doubts that deliverance is a miracle, he should read Mark 9:38-39, Acts 8:6-7 and 19:11-12 to be persuaded. Deliverance and divine healing are complementary ministries that ought to be practiced in that order for greater effectiveness.

The restoration of this woman produced a hostile reaction on the part of the leader of this synagogue, who objected to Jesus doing a work of this kind on the Sabbath, thus breaking Jewish traditions about the keeping of the day of rest. Jesus, perhaps angered by his lack of mercy, answered:

And ought not this woman, being a daughter of Abraham, whom Satan hath bound, lo, these eighteen years, be loosed from this bond on the Sabbath day?

This statement indicates that the illness that plagued this woman's body was not natural, but supernatural, actually caused by the presence in her body of a spirit of infirmity which atrophied her spine. The woman definitely was not a hypochondriac; neither was her sickness psychosomatic in nature (as some have insinuated), but real. Satan during eighteen years had kept her "bound," placing within her this spirit of infirmity which tormented her and stripped her of her freedom.

Today in the world you can find many serious illnesses that will not respond effectively or permanently to the most sophisticated medical treatments. Doctors, specialists in their fields of medicine, many times face tremendous difficulties in trying to diagnose and cure them. The medicines they prescribe barely retard the spread and ravages of these diseases, prolonging the life of its victims for a few months or years and giving them an opportunity to more or less carry on their usual activities.

Diabetes, epilepsy, leukemia, hemophilia, multiple sclerosis, AIDS, and certain types of cancer, arthritis, paralysis, blindness, etc., are incurable diseases that have no known medical solution. In such cases, we ought to suspect that a spirit of infirmity might be operating somewhere in such physical bodies. Demons cannot be detected by taking blood tests or urine samples, but only through the gift of discerning of spirits. The presence of demons in our organism cannot be proven with X-rays or ultrasound examinations. Cardiograms, encephalograms and sonograms might indicate a serious malfunction of one of our vital organs, but they seldom reveal the true cause.

Spirits of infirmity never come out even with the most powerful drugs. Radiation, chemotherapy and other modern treatments—in spite of being so expensive and hazardous to the general health of the patients—cannot annihilate demons. Medicine is impotent to combat a demonic infection—only God's power can do that!

Jesus recognized that this woman was a "daughter of Abraham." She wasn't an evil person, dominated by bad habits. She seemed to be a devout Jewess, who attended regularly the religious functions held at the synagogue. This compels us to ask ourselves, what does it truly mean to be a son (or daughter) of Abraham? The most frequent answer I have heard is that they are persons of Jewish extraction. But to truly know what is implied in being a son of Abraham we must go to the Scriptures. The Word of God can only be interpreted correctly by comparing Scripture with Scripture.

According to Galatians 3:7, "...they which are of faith, the same are the children of Abraham." Showing due respect to this biblical declaration we must affirm that this woman was a "daughter of Abraham," not necessarily because she belonged to the Jewish race, but because she was a genuine believer, that in the likeness of Abraham, the father of faith, she believed God (Romans 4:11,16; 9:7-8). We too are the "seed" (issue, progeny, offspring, lineage, descendants) of Abraham (Galatians 3:29), for we belong to Christ, who according to verse 16 of the same chapter is the true seed of Abraham. As Abraham's rightful heirs, we have the privilege and prerogative of claiming all the promises contained in the Abrahamic covenant, including healing (Deuteronomy 7:12-15) and deliverance (Luke 1:71-75).

This case serves to prove once again that even true believers (those who believe God and His Word) can be invaded in some part of their body or soul by evil spirits, and, therefore, need to submit to an anointed ministry, that with the authority and experience acquired through the years can set them free from such cruel bondage.

CASE #5

ANANIAS AND SAPPHIRA

"...Why hath Satan filled thine heart, to lie to the Holy Ghost... ?"
—Acts 5:3—

The Church of the first century was experiencing revival. The continuous manifestation of the Holy Spirit kindled within the Church a sincere desire to help the poor and needy. The disciples sold their possessions (lands and houses) and brought the proceeds to the apostles, who distributed them in an honest and equitable manner among the poverty-stricken members of the church and the community (Acts 4:34-35).

Ananias and his wife Sapphira, members in good standing of the Jerusalem church, didn't want to be the exception. Imitating other donors, they decided to sell a piece of property and donate the receipts. It is quite probable that during the transaction they received more than expected. Once they were in possession of the money, they devised a plan to deceive the apostles, deciding to give only part but pretending that it was the full amount. This action was sheer deception and hypocrisy.

Ananias, with the bag of money in his hand, met with Peter, expecting to be applauded for his liberality, but things didn't turn out as he expected. With scathing words, Peter reproached Ananias for his attempt to deceive, not merely man, but God Himself:

Ananias, why hath Satan filled thine heart to lie to the Holy Ghost ... Why hast thou conceived this thing in thine heart? Thou hast not lied unto men, but unto God?

These words reveal that Ananias, in his deliberate attempt to deceive Peter (and consequently God), was being influenced by Satan, who had succeeded in entering his heart, sowing there the idea of carrying out such a despicable act. The word "filled" (Gr. *pleroo*) is the same word that appears in Ephesians 5:18, where it refers to the infilling or fulness of the Holy Spirit. Satan wasn't influencing Ananias from the outside, but from the inside.

Although Ananias had been instigated by Satan to consummate this deed, he was entirely responsible for his actions. This scheme was fully premeditated. He and his wife had agreed to deceive the apostles. He couldn't say, as many often do (when they try to acquit themselves of all guilt), that "the devil made me do it," for he was doing this in full control of his mental capabilities. Proof of this is that he had to pay dearly for his audacity. As a result, he dropped dead and was buried without being mourned. Sapphira, his wife, suffered the same fate (5:10), which serves to prove that an accomplice is equally guilty before God as the perpetrator (Romans 1:32).

Cases #1-4 occurred before Calvary and Pentecost, which has been used by some to assert that these persons had not experienced the new birth and, therefore, were still, susceptible to evil spirits. But the case we have just considered took place after the outpouring of the Spirit on the day of Pentecost, even while the Holy Spirit was operating freely and powerfully in the Church, regenerating, transforming and liberating those who repented and gave their hearts to Jesus. Ananias and Sapphira were doubtlessly true believers, for otherwise they would have not have qualified as a part of the church in Jerusalem. In those days, only persons who had given ample evidence of their conversion were permitted to attend the meetings held at the temple or in the homes of the early disciples.

CASE #6

SIMON THE MAGICIAN

"For I perceive that thou art in the gall of bitterness, and in the bond of iniquity"
—Acts 8:23—

One of the cases that might create a great deal of controversy is that of Simon the Magician, described in Acts 8:9:24. Simon was a skilled practitioner of the occult sciences, who for quite some time had exercised his profession as a fortune-teller or sorcerer in the city of Samaria. According to the Scriptures, he had deceived the Samaritans pretending to be "some great one." The residents in that city attributed his "miracles" (lying wonders) to "the great power of God." He had worked with such cleverness that all, from "the least to the greatest," believed that he was God's anointed.

The Word emphatically affirms that Simon, with his magical arts, had "bewitched" the Samaritans. It isn't strange then to know that, according to Acts 8:7, there were many demoniacs in that city, together with many that suffered from crippling diseases, in some cases as a direct result of the curses or spells that Simon had cast on individuals or whole families at the request of some of his clients.

When Phillip—one of the seven servants or deacons of the church at Jerusalem (Acts 6:3-5) and a future evangelist (Acts 21:8)—went down to Samaria (because of the persecution that broke out as a result of Stephen's martyrdom), he faced a hostile atmosphere, both racially and spiritually. Without fear or hesitation, he began to preach the Gospel of the Kingdom (Acts 8:12) with God's endorsement through "signs and wonders." Many persons, affected body and soul by evil spirits, were delivered, healed and fully restored. Upon seeing the manifestation of God's power through Phillip's life and ministry, the Samaritans converted to Christ en mass and, in obedience to the Word, were baptized.

The Bible says: "Then Simon himself believed also: and when he was baptized, he continued with Phillip" (Acts 8:13). Although some Bible commentators have expressed their doubts or reservations as to Simon's sincerity when he "believed," apparently he fulfilled the basic requirements to be saved established in Mark 16:16, where it literally says: "He that believeth and is baptized shall be saved." After his conversion Simon "attached himself to Phillip" (TCNT) or "was constantly in Phillip's company" (NEB) or "remained in close attendance on Phillip" (WEY), causing us to understand that he had become Phillip's assistant in ministry. Knowing that Phillip had an itinerant ministry, perhaps he was hoping that some day he might become the pastor of that emerging church, and thus recover the widespread influence he had lost.

It has been suggested that Satan had planted him in that church under formation to stymie God's work and to bring it to naught. This wouldn't be at all strange, for through the centuries "infiltration" has been one of our enemy's favorite tactics to weaken the Church of Jesus Christ (Galatians 2:4; 2 Peter 2:1; Judas 4; Revelation 2:20-23).

Only God knows if Simon's conversion was wholehearted. What is quite evident, though, is that he was never delivered from the evil forces that operated in his inner being as a result of his deep involvement in the occult. Perhaps Phillip, due to his lack of experience in the ministry of the Spirit, was unable to discern that Simon was still under a strong demonic influence. A visit by the apostles Peter and John was required to expose what was truly in Simon's heart (Acts 8:20-23). Peter urged him to repent. If he would have heeded this advice, he would been delivered from the "gall of bitterness and ... the bond of iniquity" that held him fast.

Whether Simon was a true believer in Christ or not, we must conclude that believers, who before salvation were involved in one way or another in the occult sciences, desperately need deliverance since demons that entered at their bidding will not leave unless they are insistently ordered out in the mighty name of Jesus.

CASE #7

TIMOTHY

"For God has not given us the spirit of fear;
but of power, and of love, and of a sound mind"
—2 Timothy 1:7—

Following the pattern established by Christ, the apostle Paul, during his long missionary career, formed many disciples that studied, traveled and ministered with him. After a long period of training, these men became powerful servants of God that took the Gospel of the Kingdom to many parts of the old Roman Empire. Among his disciples there was one, called Timothy, that eventually became his favorite. Paul testifies to this fact when in Philippians 2:19-20 he says that no one was so "like-minded" (compatible or congenial) as Timothy.

Paul had met him in a city called Lystra during his second missionary trip (Acts 16:1-3). Timothy was a remarkable young man, highly recommended by the brethren of that church and city. Paul immediately recognized God's calling and anointing upon his life, and for that reason he invited him to accompany him during the rest of his long journey. Because of the trust that developed between them, years later Paul left Timothy in Ephesus to set the church in order (1 Timothy 1:3). Some believe that Timothy became the first pastor of that church, which has been considered the most spiritual and mature of New Testament times. There are evidences that

Timothy later became an apostle (compare 1 Thessalonians 2:6 with 1:1).

In 2 Timothy 1:6, Paul admonishes his young disciple to "stir up" (kindle, activate, awaken, revive, etc.) the gift that he had received from God through the laying on of the hands of the apostle. Apparently, Timothy had neglected this gift to the point that only some dying embers remained. What was the gift that Paul referred to? Was it one of the spiritual gifts (charismas) mentioned in 1 Corinthians 12:4,7-11? Or was it one of the ministerial gifts (offices) mentioned in Ephesians 4:8,11-12?

Although the Bible is not precise in identifying this gift, we can conclude that possibly it was the ministry of a prophet, for in 2 Timothy 1:8 Paul advises him to not be ashamed of the "testimony of our Lord." According to Revelation 19:10, "the testimony of Jesus is the spirit of prophecy" that operated in the prophets. It is evident that Timothy had not developed or used this precious gift or ministry, because there was a serious hindrance in his personal life that Paul identified as "the spirit of fear."

The Bible teaches us in Romans 8:15 that fear is caused by an evil spirit:

For ye have not received the spirit of bondage again to fear...

This spirit must be "cast out," just like any other spirit (1 John 4:18). Luke 1:74-75 says that the coming Messiah, in fulfillment of the Abrahamic covenant, was going to deliver His people from all their enemies (in our case, demons), so that "without fear" we might serve God "in holiness and righteousness...all the days of our life." According to Proverbs 29:25, "The fear of man bringeth a snare," which means that fear (any type of fear) binds or captivates, making it impossible for you and me to develop or express ourselves as we ought to. These verses prove that fear hinders us from serving God as He requires.

According to Hebrews 2:14-15, it was necessary for the Son of God to partake of "flesh and blood" that "through death he might destroy him that had the power of death, that is, the devil" and, therefore, "deliver them who through fear of death were all their lifetime subject to bondage." Fear—and especially this universal fear, the fear of death—"subjects to bondage," that is, it subjugates, imprisons, enslaves.

Timothy, although God's servant, was affected by a spirit of fear, that aroused within him feelings of inferiority, timidity, indecision, shame, cowardice, mistrust, etc. It is probable that this spirit entered him while he was yet a child, for there is evidence that he had been brought up in a divided or dysfunctional home. The Scriptures teach us that Timothy was the son of a devout Jewish mother and of a Greek father (unconverted?) that perhaps took little or no interest in his son's moral and spiritual development. Two godly women, his mother Eunice and his grandmother Lois, had taught him from his earliest years the Holy Scriptures (2 Timothy 3:15) and had sowed within him genuine faith in God (2

Timothy 1:5).

In spite of such excellent moral and biblical training, Timothy had a serious problem which explains why he had not been able to develop a solid and stable personality which would have permitted him to act with confidence and aplomb in the face of adversity. Knowing by the writings of the Old Testament that the prophetic ministry many times stirs up fierce opposition, Timothy, consumed by fear, had chosen to set his gift aside, and not risk the possibility of facing persecution and death.

If Timothy, a young minister of such impeccable credentials, had at least one demonic problem that he had to face and overcome, how can you affirm (as many often do) that you have no problems of that nature, "for Christians cannot have demons," as perhaps you have been erroneously taught.

THE APOSTLE PAUL

**"And lest I should be exalted above measure
through the abundance of revelations, there
was given to me a thorn in the flesh, the
messenger of Satan, to buffet me, lest
I should be exalted above measure"
—2 Corinthians 12:7—**

Many Christian will think it strange to include Paul in the list of persons that in some period of their existence were strongly influenced by evil spirits, for he has been placed upon a pedestal by evangelical Christians worldwide. Paul is considered "untouchable" by many present-day Protestants, for they have nearly the same veneration for him, the Catholics do for Peter.

Despite his great personal merits and achievements, we must be willing to admit that Paul as a human being was subject to the temptations and passions that are common to all men (1 Corinthians 10:13; James 5:17). Therefore, I beg the readers to keep an open heart and mind while we examine some Bible passages that lead to the conviction that Paul also was affected in the inward part of his being by evil spirits.

It is undeniable that Paul was not only an apostle but also a prophet. As such, he had great and, sometimes, strange manifestations of the Spirit (such as visions and trances) that are frequent in the prophetic ministry. For example, Paul in Acts 22:17-21 testifies that at the beginning of his Christian life, praying in the temple at Jerusalem, "I was in a trance" or ecstasy. The Spanish equivalent to the King James Bible says: "I was caught up" or "I was raptured out of myself," which would seem to imply that it was an out-of-body experience. During this mystical happening, Paul saw the Lord Jesus, who gave him direct and urgent orders to leave Jerusalem because his life was in danger.

Paul, as prophet, had the ability of leaving his body in spirit at the urging of the Holy Spirit. This experience also occurred in the life of other servants of God, both in the Old and New Testaments, such as Elisha (2 Kings 5:25-26), Ezekiel (Ezekiel 8:1-3), Peter (Acts 10:10-17) and John (Revelation 4:1-2; 17:1-3; 21:9-10). Due to the fact that in spiritualism similar experiences—called "astral projection" or "cosmic flight"—are common-place, the contemporary church tends to reject them completely.

In 2 Corinthians 12:1-9, Paul describes an experience in which he was caught up to the "third heaven" or "paradise," where he "heard unspeakable words, which it is not lawful for a man to utter." This happening was so real and mind-boggling, that Paul wasn't sure whether it had been "in the body" or "out of the body." Unfortunately, the person that has this type of experiences tends to exalt himself unduly. Paul was no exception. According to his own confession, in him there was a proclivity towards spiritual pride and, as Proverbs 16:18

says, "Pride goeth before destruction."

As a preventative measure, to avoid failure in his personal life and ministry, there was given unto him a "thorn in the flesh, the messenger of Satan," to buffet him, so that he would not exalt himself excessively. Among many other things, the dictionary defines the word "thorn" as: prick, spur, goad; a pointed instrument to pierce or puncture; anything that annoys and torments sharply.

According to Paul this "thorn" operated in his "flesh." The word "flesh" in the Bible can refer to at least these three different things:

1) The matter or substance that makes up the physical body (Luke 24:39; 1 Corinthians 15:50);
2) The human being or race (Acts 2:17; Matthew 24:22); and
3) The fallen, corrupt, depraved human nature (Romans 8:5-8; Galatians 5:16-17).

It is necessary to examine carefully the context of each passage of Scripture where the word "flesh" appears, in order to determine correctly to which of these three options the author was making allusion. In the case we are concerned with, it seems safe to say that Paul is talking about his body or, perhaps, his sinful nature.

In 2 Corinthians 11:29, Paul says: "Who is weak, and I am not weak?" The word "weak" used here is *astheneo*, which according to Strong's concordance can mean:

"weak, feeble, sick, diseased or impotent." This verse causes us to understand that all human beings (including Paul) are susceptible to weakness or disease. Some students of the Word believe that Paul suffered from a chronic eye disease, and for that reason he wasn't able to write his own epistles but used a clerk (ghost writer?) instead. At the end he would add a short greeting or his signature (Romans 16:22; Galatians 6:11; 1 Corinthians 16:21; Colossians 4:18; 2 Thessalonians 3:17). They also affirm that it was for that reason that some believers in the Galatian churches were willing to take out their eyes, if possible, and donate them to him (Galatians 4:15). Other writers have suggested that Paul had a speech impediment; that he stuttered badly (2 Corinthians 10:10) and, therefore, his messages were long and tedious (Acts 20:7,11).

There are others that suggest that Paul had a moral problem, a weakness or tendency towards a certain sin of the flesh, that forced him to be in a constant state of alert in order to not commit a sin that would destroy the effectiveness of his testimony and ministry. Some writers, that represent the liberal wing of the Christian church, have even insinuated that Paul had homosexual tendencies and that for such a reason he had never married (1 Corinthians 7:7-8).

We cannot ascertain which of these interpretations is the correct one, but we can be sure that his condition (whether it was a physical illness or a moral weakness) was caused by "a messenger of Satan" that operated in his "flesh." The word "messenger" in the Greek, the language in which the New Testament was written, is *aggelos*, that can be translated either angel or messenger. The context will determine if it refers to a spiritual entity or to a human being who is the bearer of a message.

Many Bible teachers assert that the "messenger of Satan" was a group of Judaizers (Jews that had converted to Christ but who had never renounced their Jewish traditions, and, therefore, required that the Gentile converts submit to the rite of circumcision, keep the Sabbath and observe certain Mosaic laws) that followed Paul everywhere contradicting his teachings and inciting the Jews to reject his ministry.

Personally, I'm convinced that "the messenger of Satan" was an angel at Satan's service (Matthew 25:41; Revelation 12:7). A great majority of Christian theologians believe that the angels which (according to them) joined Lucifer in his rebellion against God at the beginning of creation, today are the demons or evil spirits that we are called to combat. I tend to think that demons and fallen angels are a different kind of spiritual beings, although equally wicked and malevolent, that serve Satan in his continuous opposition to God and His people.

The "messenger of Satan" that attacked Paul (or operated in him), buffeted or battered him when he manifested pride and arrogance due to the divine revelations he had received. God, and not Satan, had given him this "thorn" to deliver him from a fall that would have brought ruin and destruction to his ministry. Three times Paul had begged God to remove this encumbrance from him, but God counseled him: "My grace is sufficient for thee; for my strength is made perfect in weakness."

To many it might seem inconceivable that God should "send" evil spirits to discipline or chastise His people, but there are enough biblical evidences to affirm that this is true (Judges 9:23; 1 Samuel 16:14; 18:10; 19:9; Proverbs 17:11). It is necessary to recognize that demons are under God's dominion and control, and that they can do nothing without His knowledge and permission. In order to understand this biblical principle, you must read carefully the stories of Job in Job chapters 1 and 2, and of the Gadarean demoniac in Mark 5:9-13. In reality, Satan and his demons are sometimes the very instruments that God uses to punish individuals, families, societies and entire nations.

"And now, behold, I go bound in the spirit unto Jerusalem"
—Acts 20:22—

During his third missionary journey, and after having ministered with great success in the city of Ephesus (that great pagan religious center renown for the majestic temple dedicated to the goddess Diana, one of the seven marvels of the ancient world), Paul "purposed in the spirit" (Acts 19:21) to go back to Jerusalem, in spite of the fact that he knew that the Lord wanted to take him in the opposite direction, to Rome and Spain (Romans 1:13,15; 15:28). Without consulting anyone, Paul embarked on the trip, visiting on the way some of the churches he had founded in Macedonia and Achaia. This act of self-determination—manifested by the words "purposed" (Acts 20:3) and "determined" (Acts 20:16) —proves that Paul had a strong will and an inflexible personality. Probably this trait was necessary in order to endure and overcome the relentless opposition of Satan and evil men that he confronted during his extensive ministry.

Feeling a vehement desire to be in Jerusalem for the feast of Pentecost, Paul decided to bypass Ephesus. Instead, he asked the elders of the church in that city to meet him at a nearby port called Miletus. During this brief encounter, Paul candidly confessed that "bound in the spirit" he was going to Jerusalem, in spite of the fact that in many cities the Holy Spirit had warned him that he would be facing imprisonment and tribulation (Acts 20:22,23). Here we must pause for a moment to ask ourselves "what" or "whom" was binding Paul in the (human) spirit to undertake this hazardous expedition, evidently by an act of self-initiative or self-determin-ation. Was it the Holy Spirit that was guiding him? or, was it an evil spirit that was obsessing him with the idea of going to Jerusalem no matter what might happen there?

Subsequently, Paul disembarked in the port of Tyre, where he spent seven days with a group of disciples who, according to Acts 21:4, told Paul "through the Spirit, that he should not go up to Jerusalem." Ignoring this clear divine prohibition, he continued his journey to Jerusalem, giving evidence that by then "something" was working in him that prodded, coerced or drove him to go. In all honesty, we ought to ask ourselves, what was the source of this compulsive behavior. If the Holy Spirit was compelling him to undertake this trip (as most Bible scholars affirm) then why so many misgivings and prohibitions? Does God contradict Himself? (2 Timothy 2:13).

Days later Paul arrived in Caesarea with his traveling companions, where God made one last-ditch effort to stop him in his tracks. During his stopover in the home of Phillip the evangelist (Acts 21:8-14), a man named Agabus (perhaps the most outstanding prophet of the early church), dropped by unannounced to see him. During one of the meetings of the local church, Agabus took Paul's belt to tie himself hand and foot, announcing through this object lesson his upcoming arrest in Jerusalem. Everyone present understood the message and begged Paul insistently to give up such an ill-fated plan. Notwithstanding, Paul, determined as ever to do what he believed (mistakenly) to be God's will, decided to go ahead regardless of the consequences. His words in Acts 21:13 might reveal a spirit of self-sufficiency and boasting already at work in him.

As soon as he got to Jerusalem, Paul presented himself to James, the head elder (equivalent to pastor) of the local assembly, who convened the rest of the elders for an urgent meeting. After the usual greetings and reports, the leaders of the church informed Paul that there was a "complot" against him, for it was widely rumored that he encouraged the Jews everywhere to turn their backs on the rite of circumcision and the observance of the Mosaic laws (Acts 21:21). In order to calm the heated tempers, James suggested that together with four other brethren of the congregation who had made a vow, Paul ought to shave his head and subject himself to a rite of purification, that included offering a sacrifice in the Jewish temple for the benefit of each one of them. Actually, they were asking him to compromise his most cherished personal convictions.

By blindly accepting and carrying out the "sound advice" of James and the elders, Paul virtually reverted to Judaism, becoming a "transgressor" according to his own words in Galatians 2:18. By not submitting to the Holy Spirit and to the legitimate spiritual authority of His peers (such as Phillip and Agabus) and his traveling companions (Trophimus and Luke, among many others), Paul ended up submitting to the doubtful authority of James and the elders, considered the main representatives of the most legalistic and sectarian wing of the first century Church.

When he entered the Jewish temple, Paul fell into a trap that Satan unquestionably had set, for he was recognized by some of his avowed enemies, who immediately arrested him and began to beat him. If it had not been for the opportune intervention of a group of Roman soldiers he could have been lynched. Sent to jail and later put on trial, Paul felt constrained to reveal that he was a Roman citizen, which naturally granted him certain prerogatives.

Days later, a conspiracy against him came to light. More than forty men had sworn under a curse that they would neither eat nor drink until they killed him (Acts 23:12-22). When Paul heard about this, alarmed he appealed to the military authorities who had incarcerated him, placing himself under the protection of the Roman Empire. Where was his bravery and determination to suffer and die, if necessary, for Christ? (read again Acts 21:13).

During this long process, Paul appealed to Caesar (Acts 25:11), which only served to further complicate his situation. Felix and Festus, governors of that Roman province, asserted that he could have been released, if he had not taken advantage of this legal recourse (Acts 25:25; 26:32). As a result, he was sent to Rome as a felon, where he was only able to minister to a few persons that dropped by to see him in the rented house that served him as prison (Acts 28:16-31). His public ministry virtually came to an end.

Although Catholic tradition teaches that Paul was liberated for a season, during which time he traveled and ministered as before, there is not a shred of biblical evidence that this might have happened.

We must recognize that in spite of everything, God's will (revealed in Acts 9:15) was fulfilled in Paul's life, although it is also quite evident that the enemy tried to hinder it at all cost, taking advantage of Paul's natural propensity toward stubbornness or obstinacy (which in most cases is the same as rebellion).

After analyzing and interpreting this long biblical passage (Acts chapters 20 to 28), can we in all justice come to the conclusion that even great leaders, such as the apostle Paul, could be affected in their innermost being by evil spirits that would seek to mess up their lives and thwart their ministries? If this is true, don't you believe that you, as a member or minister of the Body of Christ, must also keep sober and vigilant knowing that your tenacious enemy, the devil (1 Peter 5:8), will sooner or later attack you subtly with the purpose of deceiving you, therefore delaying or obstructing, at least in part, God's purposes for you, your family and church, and, consequently, for all of mankind?

SECTION III

Proof Texts:
Bible Passages Which Prove
That A Christian Can Be
Contaminated
By Demons

I am now going to deal carefully with some portions of Scripture that help prove that a Christian can be invaded and bound by evil spirits. No single, isolated passage is sufficient in itself to establish an irrefutable doctrinal position. We must study each passage in relation to its context and with other texts that enlarge upon the same subject.

TEXT #1

"...if ye receive another spirit, which ye have not received..."
—2 Corinthians 11:34—

Corinth was doubtlessly one of the churches where the Holy Spirit could manifest Himself with greatest freedom in New Testament times. In spite of some severe problems that were beginning to come to light in this church (rivalries, immorality, drunkenness, doctrinal deviations, etc.), the Holy Spirit was able to work powerfully through some of the gifts which He had imparted (1 Corinthians 1:4-8).

Due to their noticeable tendency towards mysticism, Paul feared that the Corinthians would be seduced by the serpent, Satan, as Eve was at the beginning of time. According to Genesis 3:1-6, the woman became an easy prey of the devil, when she twisted or misinterpreted God's message to Adam, forbidding him to eat of the tree of good and evil. In the same way, Paul was alerting the Corinthian believers that they also could permit themselves to be deceived by their lack of a personal and profound knowledge of the Word of God.

Satan had planted several of his emissaries in the early Church—false apostles (2 Corinthians 11:13), false prophets (I John 4:1) and false teachers (2 Peter 2:1) —whose main job was to propagate false doctrines (1 Timothy 1:3) with the purpose of overthrowing the faith of the new converts (2 Timothy 2:18). To achieve this shameful objective these false ministers offered "another Jesus," communicated "another spirit" and preached "another Gospel." If they submitted blindly to the teaching and ministry of these impostors, not discerning the spirit that operated in them, the Corinthians were in danger of drifting away from the truth, to the point that they could fall into apostasy (1 Timothy 4:1).

It is evident that one of the greatest risks faced by the members of the church at Corinth was receiving "another spirit," entirely different from the one they had already received (i.e. the Holy Spirit).

Other versions of the Bible translate this verse as follows:

If you receive a different spirit from the one you received (NIV).

When you are treated to a spirit different from the Spirit you once received (MOF).

You readily receive a spirit ... quite different from the (one) *you originally accepted* (PHIL).

If you then receive a spirit different from the Spirit already given you (NEB).

Though it was obvious that the Corinthians had received the Holy Spirit, there was yet a possibility that another spirit could infiltrate them. If this happened, the results would be disastrous for them. Their spiritual senses would be corrupted and impaired, which would cause them to depart from their sincere and faithful devotion to Christ.

Today we face the same dangers that the believers of the first century faced, for Satan, using one of his favorite tactics, has infiltrated many churches, even those that claim to be "renewed in the Spirit." Ministers endowed with a magnetic personality travel all over the world preaching a popular gospel and communicating by the laying on of hands (and other more questionable methods, such as blowing, pushing, etc.) "another spirit" of a religious nature. It is of utmost importance today, more than at any other time in church history, that we be wary of certain persons that seem so anxious to lay hands on us "lightly" (1 Timothy 5:22). If we let them do it, they probably will communicate "another spirit" to us that would cause severe damage to our doctrinal beliefs, morals and physical and mental health.

TEXT #2

"Neither give place to the devil"
—Ephesians 4:27—

This verse, one of the shortest of the whole Bible, contains a clear-cut order given by the Apostle Paul to the

Ephesian believers to not "give place" (opportunity) to the devil to work in, or amongst them. Other versions are even more arresting:

Don't give the devil that sort of foothold (PHIL).

Leave no loop-hole for the devil (NEB).

And don't give the devil a chance (CONT).

If there wasn't a real possibility or an imminent danger of the devil's finding a convenient place to lodge in us, I doubt that the Holy Spirit would have issued such a warning through Paul. Experience proves that the enemy is going to occupy any territory we relinquish or surrender to him.

When we give free rein to our flesh, when we indulge our carnal nature, we give the devil suitable grounds on which to work freely among us, or in us. In Ephesians 4:25-26, 28-29, 31, we find some of the works of the flesh that open doors so the devil can enter and operate in us: lying, anger, stealing, obscenity, bitterness, slander, etc. Any unconfessed sin, no matter how trivial it might seem, gives the enemy a legal right to invade our being. Therefore, it is extremely important that we keep our accounts short with God and our fellowman.

An example of how this principle operates can be found in verse 26 of Ephesians 4, where Paul, speaking about anger, gives wise advice: "Let not the sun go down upon your wrath." If during the daytime hours you have had a strong disagreement or heated discussion with your spouse or with some other person close to you, you should not retire for the night without resolving your differences, for "while men slept, his enemy came and sowed tares" (Matthew 13:25) and tares are "the children of the wicked one" (Matthew 13:38). That means that in order to keep the enemy from sowing "tares" (demons?) in you, you must settle accounts daily. According to Proverbs 22:24-25, anger is a "snare" to your soul. Letting this sin fester and grow in your heart is a deadly trap that could destroy your own life (Job 5:2).

The flesh is called "the body of sin" or "the body of this death" in Paul's writings (Romans 6:6 and 7:24, respectively). Paul compares the flesh—our corrupt, depraved human nature—with a carcass (a dead and decaying body). The corpse of a man or an animal attracts the attention of birds of prey (eagles, falcons, owls, vultures, etc.) that habitually feed on putrid flesh.

The "fowls of the air" mentioned in the parable of the sower (Mark 4:4,15; Luke 8:5,12) represent, according to Bible typology, Satan and his demons. Jesus said that "wheresoever the carcass is, there will the eagles be gathered together" (Matthew 24:28). Giving this passage a symbolic interpretation (and not its usual eschatological explanation), we can affirm without fear of being mistaken, that where the dead body (the flesh) is, there the "eagles" (Satan and his demons) are certainly going to gather.

In Genesis 15:5-18 we find an interesting story that

describes the exact moment when Jehovah God made a covenant with His friend, Abraham. In preparation for this memorable event in the life of the patriarch and his descendants, God ordered Abraham to prepare and sacrifice a number of animals and birds, in order to guarantee the fulfillment of this historic covenant. It was a custom in Israel and other countries of the Middle East for the persons that were going to enter into a covenant relationship, to slay certain animals, divide them into halves, and place the pieces face to face, leaving a passage or corridor down the middle so the "confederates" could walk together between them (Jeremiah 34:18-20). This was considered a "blood covenant," perhaps the most serious and binding of all. By doing this they were accepting the fact that in case one of them broke the covenant unilaterally he deserved to suffer the fate of the slain animals, that is death itself.

The previous Scripture also indicates that while Abraham waited for the Lord to appear on the scene, "the fowls came down upon the carcasses" of the animals and birds that Abraham had sacrificed, but he "drove them away." That means that Abraham had to stay alert to frighten away the birds of prey that attempted to devour the animals before the covenant was made. We, too, must maintain an attitude of constant watchfulness, for our flesh ("the body of this death") is going to attract the "fowls" (demons) that revolve around us seeking an opportunity to infiltrate and shatter our lives.

TEXT #3

**"...those that oppose themselves ...that they
may recover themselves out of the snare
of the devil, who are taken captive
by him at his will"
—2 Timothy 2:25-26—**

Outbreaks of rebellion were already taking place in some of the churches established by the apostle Paul in several different countries. As it happens frequently today, certain persons who believed they were more spiritual or better trained intellectually were rising up against the local elders or pastors, opposing their authority and teaching, at times even publicly. In this Bible passage, the apostle instructs his young disciple, Timothy, how to face and solve such a delicate situation.

God's servant cannot ignore or tolerate such an attitude, for "a little leaven leaveneth the whole lump" (1 Corinthians 5:6). Rebellion is an infectious disease that must be faced with meekness, but also with courage and strength. Strict (but loving) discipline must be exercised. Rebels must be placed under probation. Instruction (or correction, verse 25) is the first step to be taken. If those guilty of this sinful tendency refuse to repent and submit, then it might be necessary for the elders to take even stronger measures, such as suspending or expelling them, or (in the most extreme cases) delivering them to the devil, as suggested in 1 Corinthians 5:1-5 and 1 Timothy 1:20.

According to 2 Timothy 2:26, believers in open rebellion towards their spiritual leaders are bound or enslaved by the devil. Therefore, they have lost their liberty to act in conformity to God's will and are under a heavy demonic oppression that forces them to do Satan's bidding. According to some recent versions of the Bible, rebels need to "come to their senses" (NASB and NKJV), that is, they need to recover their soberness or sanity. Not only their will is imprisoned, but, in most cases, their mind is muddled and controlled by the devil.

According to 1 Samuel 15:23, rebellion before God is as serious an offense as divination or sorcery. Rebels end up consorting with the devil. Rebellion attracts demons the same way that magnets attract metals. In Proverbs 17:11 we find that:

An evil man seeketh only rebellion: therefore a cruel messenger shall be sent against him.

Rebellion is born in an evil heart. It brings dire consequences on the offender and his descendants. The word "messenger" in the Hebrew is *mal-awk*, which in the majority of cases in the Old Testament is translated "angel." This "cruel messenger," then, is a fallen angel, merciless, malevolent, ruthless, sadistic, that is going to vent his fury on the person that falls into his hands.

A typical example of this principle can be found in the life of king Saul, who on two different occasions disobeyed divine orders given through God's servant, Samuel (1 Samuel 13:13-14; 15:2-3). As a result of his rebellion, the Holy Spirit departed from him and an evil spirit from God began to torment him (1 Samuel 16:14), in such a way that in due time Saul developed all the symptoms of a manic-depressive. His end was certainly tragic, for he wound up taking his own life. In 1 Chronicles 10:13 it says:

So Saul died for his transgression (rebellion) which he committed against the Lord, even against the word of the Lord, which he kept not, and also for asking counsel of one that had a familiar spirit, to inquire of it.

Also, in Isaiah 63:10 we find that through rebellion the children of Israel "vexed (grieved) his holy Spirit," and therefore He became their enemy, and, instead of favoring them, He "fought against them." According to James 4:4, becoming friends of the world—which is evident when you adopt its fashions, pleasures, musical styles, etc.—is an act of rebellion towards God, by which you end up becoming His enemy.

The system that is ruling the world today is in manifest rebellion against God (1 John 5:19), and if you partake of it you risk His wrath. You should not be overly concerned with having Satan as your enemy, because with the authority of Jesus Christ you can resist, bind and defeat him. But under no circumstances should you countenance having as an enemy the Holy Spirit, who as God will never submit Himself to you. The greatest danger rebels face is that the Holy Spirit might rise up against them and destroy the works of their hands

(Ecclesiastes 5:6). Is that the reason why so many believers and ministers, though they work hard and battle doggedly, never prosper?

In Ephesians 2:2-3, we also read:

Wherein in time past ye walked according to the course of this world, according to the prince of the power of the air, the spirit that now worketh in the children of disobedience.

According to this verse, the persons that claim to be Christians but live in avowed opposition to the will of God are called "children of disobedience" (see also Colossians 3:6). Living "in the lusts of our flesh, fulfilling the desires of the flesh and of the mind," they have opened themselves up to the manifestation of an evil spirit, not just a minor spirit, but a real principality, called in this case "the prince of the power of the air." Disobedience or rebellion gives this satanic "strong man" (Matthew 12:29) the right to work in and through you.

The persons that are in rebellion toward God, and also toward the human authorities which He has placed as a covering over them, urgently need to repent so they can "know the truth" (John 8:32) and "recover themselves (or escape) out of the snare of the devil" in which they are held "captive by him at his will." Rebels also need to submit to a deliverance prayer so their bondages can be broken by the power of the Holy Spirit and thus they can be free from the demons that plague their bodies and their souls.

"... the things which the Gentiles sacrifice,
they sacrifice to devils, and not to God:
and I would not that ye should have
fellowship with devils"
—1 Corinthians 10:20—

The Bible teaches us that when we partake of the Lord's Table—called by some Communion and, by others, the Eucharist—we participate of the body and blood of Jesus Christ. Through these elements we receive divine "blessing" (1 Corinthians 10: 16). Although I don't consider biblically acceptable the Catholic doctrine of "transubstantiation"—that when the host and the wine are elevated and consecrated by the priest they literally become the body and blood of Christ—I do believe that something real, tangible and meaningful takes place when the Christian minister prays over the elements and blesses them. In effect, the bread and the wine are imbued with the benefits of Christ's atoning work on Calvary.

If this be true, the Lord's Supper ceases being merely a memorial (1 Corinthians 11:26, "ye do shew the Lord's death till he come") and becomes a sublime experience as the believer by the Spirit partakes of Christ and His redemptive work. When he partakes of the Lord's Table in faith, the believer can receive, among other things, health for his physical body. During more than 40 years of ministry I have seen many persons healed— miraculously and instantaneously—as they took

Communion, not as a religious observance but as a personal encounter with Christ.

In like fashion, when a believer in disobedience to God participates of things sacrificed to idols, he receives "cursing," because he participates of the demons that reside in those idols (Leviticus 17:7; Deuteronomy 32:17; Psalm 106:36-37; Revelation 9:20). Eating meats sacrificed to idols results in spiritual "pollution" (Acts 15:20) or "defilement" (1 Corinthians 8:7; Ezekiel 20:7,18; 22:3-4; 37:23).

According to Acts 15:1-29, during the first Church council held in Jerusalem, the apostles and elders present at the meeting had to deal with this matter, for there was compelling evidence that many believers were being affected by eating this type of meat. According to ecclesiastical history, many ancient heathen temples had opened butchershops (meat markets) to sell at a reduced price the meats that were left over from the sacrifices to their gods. The believers, mostly from the poorest classes of society, took advantage of the opportunity to buy "prime cuts" at bargain prices, without suspecting that these same meats were contaminated with the evil spirits that indwelt the idols. When they ate these meats they were literally "eating demons."

After lengthy discussions, those in attendance at the council of Jerusalem, under the guidance of the Holy Spirit (verse 28), issued a decree—still valid today—ordering all believers, Jews and Gentiles alike, to "abstain from meats sacrificed to idols, and from blood, and from things strangled, and from fornication" (verse 29). Even today through these four things, human beings can be infected, not only by bacteria, germs, microbes and viruses, but by demons.

To avoid spiritual contamination through foodstuffs, it is recommended that before we ingest them we sanctify them by prayer and thanksgiving (1 Timothy 4:4-5), and especially when they are from a dubious or unknown source. This is particularly true when we are invited to eat at a restaurant where foreign or exotic foods are served (have you noticed how prevalent dragons are in the decor of most Chinese restaurants?) or in the home of unbelievers that might be somehow involved in the occult. Using our authority in Christ, we can break any curse that has been placed upon that food.

As a result of fornication—that, in a generic sense, is any type of "unlawful sexual intercourse" (premarital or extramarital), including adultery, homosexuality, bestiality, etc.—you can transmit not only venereal diseases, such as gonorrhea, genital herpes, syphilis and even AIDS, but also evil spirits that will not only affect man's health and morals, but even his spiritual life. Illicit or deviant sexual relationships are one of the easiest, and most common, means of defiling, contaminating or polluting both body and soul (Leviticus 18:20,23-24; Ezekiel 23:11-14,17; Matthew 15:19-20). According to 1 Timothy 1:10, whoremongers (fornicators) and sodomites (homosexuals) "defile themselves with mankind." The Bible plainly says that "he that committeth fornication sinneth against his own body" (1Corinthians

6:18) and that in himself he will receive "that recompence of their error which was meet (proper, fitting)" (Romans 1:27). Or, as another version puts it, they will receive "the fitting wage of their own perversion" (NEB).

When the council ordered Christians to abstain "from blood," it referred not only to the blood of animals —which in some countries the natives drink when they slaughter their cattle or eat in the form of a "blood sausage"—but all types, including human blood. Blood transfusions can be a means of direct contagion, for it has been proven scientifically that through contaminated blood injected directly into the veins you can transmit incurable and even deadly diseases, such as pernicious anemia, leukemia, hepatitis B, AIDS and others, that in many cases are caused by evil spirits.

It is undeniable that disobedience to certain divine principles, both in the Old and New Testaments, can open us up to a contamination of demons which will seriously affect all the aspects of our personal life, both naturally and spiritually. These laws were given by God for our protection and when we violate them we make ourselves vulnerable to grave dangers which proceed from the spiritual world of darkness and death that surrounds us.

"To deliver such an one unto Satan for the destruction of the flesh, that the spirit may be saved in the day of the Lord Jesus"
—1 Corinthians 5:5—

A member of the church at Corinth had established an illicit sexual relationship with his stepmother. An intimate relationship of this kind was decisively forbidden by the Word of God in Leviticus 18:8 and Deuteronomy 22:30. This serious offense, called today incest, is an act of disobedience to God's laws that always brings a curse upon the transgressor (Deuteronomy 27:20). Many times demons are God's agents in carrying out a curse imposed due to man's disobedience to the Word of God.

In spite of the fact that this man's sin was widely known, the church had not taken any disciplinary action at all. There was an attitude of extreme tolerance which Paul didn't hesitate in condemning. The apostle, under the direction of the Holy Spirit, ordered the church to meet with the authority of Jesus Christ to apply proper discipline. Due to the gravity of the case, Paul proposed that they "deliver" him to Satan without hesitation or pity "for the destruction of the flesh," so that his spirit could be saved in the day of the Lord.

Although we are unaware of what really happened in the spirit world when the church legally turned this man over to the devil, we can suppose that his body was invaded by evil spirits that provoked some serious health problems that could have taken him to an early grave. The purpose of this suffering was to make him reflect about his immoral behavior and force him to change his depraved lifestyle (1 Peter 4:1-2).

No doubt the man repented, since most expositors agree that in 2 Corinthians 2:1-11 Paul refers to him when he orders the church to confirm its love to an unspecified person, forgiving, comforting and restoring him to fellowship. If they had refused to do so, the church itself would have suffered dire consequences, for Satan would have taken advantage of the opportunity thus given him to deceive and "gain an edge" over the entire congregation.

This wasn't the only time that Paul took the initiative in delivering certain persons to Satan, for in 1 Timothy 1:19-20 he did the same with Hymenaeus (who had "erred from truth," preaching a false doctrine in relation to the resurrection of the dead, 2 Timothy 2:17-18) and Alexander, the coppersmith (who did him "much evil," 2 Timothy 4:14). Both men had blasphemed and, therefore, deserved the drastic punishment that Paul meted out to them.

TEXT #6

"Even so we, when we were children, were in bondage under the elements of the world" —Galatians 4:3—

Although at first sight, this passage of Scripture doesn't describe the possible operation of evil spirits in the life of the believers in Christ, after consulting numerous versions of the Bible, both in Spanish and English, I have arrived at the conclusion that the author of the epistle makes reference to it, when he says that the spiritual "child" (the carnal believer, according to 1 Corinthians 3:1-3, Hebrews 5:12-14 and 1 Peter 2:1-2) is a servant or slave "under the elements of the world."

This verse has been translated elsewhere as follows:

And so it was with us. During our minority we were slaves to the elemental spirits of the universe (RSV & NEB).

We were slaves to the ruling spirits of the universe, before we reached spiritual maturity (GNMM).

These versions cause us to understand that in the life of a carnal Christian certain "forces" or "powers" are in operation, that want to keep him in a state of spiritual immaturity. These spirits cause his spiritual development to stagnate. They are like parasites in the digestive system of a child that devour the nutrients and interfere with his normal growth. During some of the deliverance seminars that I have participated in, I have called demons "spiritual ticks" or "leeches," insects that suck the blood of animals and keep them from gaining weight or getting fat. In the same way, demons tend to "suck" or absorb the spiritual sap of its "hosts," hindering their maturation into the image of Christ.

Satan knows that as long as he can keep the believer in spiritual infancy, he will never become a threat to his evil kingdom. A carnal Christian, under the influence or control of unclean spirits, will never be able to possess or enjoy the inheritance that rightfully belongs to him as the "seed of Abraham" (Galatians 3:29) or as a "son of God" (Galatians 4:7; Romans 8:17). Once delivered from the spiritual "parasites" that plague him, the believer can grow until he reaches the stature of the perfect man (Ephesians 4:13) and thus inherit or possess all the things that God has promised and provided for His people (Romans 8:32; 1 Corinthians 3:21; 2 Peter 1:3).

TEXT #7

**"Who opposeth and exalteth himself above all
that is called God, or that is worshipped;
so that he as God sitteth in the temple of God,
shewing himself that he is God"
—2 Thessalonians 2:4—**

Many Bible scholars—and particularly those that are specialists in the field of prophecy—believe that this well known portion of Scripture makes direct reference to a sinister personage that will appear on the world political scene in the days that precede the Second Coming of Christ. This individual—better known as the Antichrist (1 John 2:18) or the Beast (Revelation 13:1-8)—will present himself as the benefactor and protector of the people of Israel. According to this widely-held theory, he will make a covenant with Israel (Daniel 9:27) which, after three and a half years of relative peace, he will break. Immediately, he will desecrate the reconstructed temple of God in Jerusalem, demanding that both Jews and the inhabitants of the whole earth offer him worship as God. This act will constitute what the Bible calls "the abomination of desolation" (Daniel 11:31; 12:11; Matthew 24:15) and will mark the beginning of the last three and a half years of the Great Tribulation period. Time will tell if this theory, accepted unconditionally by perhaps 90% of Christians, is true or not.

Setting aside the eschatological implications of this

passage, it is important that we undertake a careful study of the term "temple of God" in the New Testament. While doing this, we will immediately discover that the authors of the New Testament, especially the apostle Paul, call believers in Christ the "temple of God," both in an individual and collective sense.

In 1 Corinthians 6:19, referring to the individual Christian, Paul says:

What? know ye not that your body is the temple of the Holy Ghost which is in you, which ye have of God...

Also, in 1 Corinthians 3:16 the same apostle affirms:

Know ye not that ye are the temple of God, and that the Spirit of God dwelleth in you?

In 2 Corinthians 6:16, referring now to the local church, he adds:

...For ye are the temple of the living God...

Paul assures us in Ephesians 2:20-22 that the universal church is the temple of God, when he declares:

And (ye) are built upon the foundation of the apostles and prophets, Jesus Christ himself being the chief corner stone; In whom all the building fitly framed together groweth unto an holy temple in the Lord... for an habitation of God through the Spirit.

The Lord Jesus Christ, speaking in John 2:19-21 about the temple, alluded figuratively to "the temple of his body." We all know according to Scripture that He not only has a physical body—in which He is seated now at the right hand of God in heaven (1 Timothy 2:5)—but also a mystical body, that is, His Church (1 Corinthians 12:12,27; Ephesians 1:22-23; Colossians 1:24), both militant (on earth) and triumphant (in heaven).

Stephen, the first martyr, declared before the Sanhedrin that "the most High dwelleth not in temples made with hands" (Acts 7:48). Paul also said, during his famous discourse on Mars' hill, that God "dwelleth not in temples made with hands" (Acts 17:24), which would force us to discard the idea that in 2 Thessalonians 2:4 he was referring to a rebuilt temple for the Jewish nation in Jerusalem in the days before the Day of the Lord. It is debatable today whether such a temple will be built before the Coming of Christ, for we lack convincing biblical evidence to confirm it. Some experts on prophecy now teach that it will not be until after the Coming of Christ that the temple will be erected in Jerusalem as a great universal worship center.

If the "temple of God" that Paul mentions in 2 Thessalonians 2:4 is either the believer, the local assembly or the universal Church, as the previous passages seem to imply, then we will be constrained to admit that such a "temple of God" can be—and will be!—invaded, violated, polluted, defiled or desecrated (1 Corinthians 3:17) by a personage called "the son of perdition." When we developed in this book some of the

New Testament cases of persons that were seized and occupied by demons, we said that Jesus called his own disciple, Judas Iscariot, "the son of perdition" (John 17:12) and indicated that he was "a devil" (or the devil himself, John 6:70). It wouldn't be surprising to discover that the "son of perdition" is a spiritual personality who manifested in Judas during the first century and who again in the last days will manifest in and through the Church.

This personage, according to Paul in 2 Thessalonians 2:4, will be characterized by his rebellion or lawlessness ("who opposseth") and pride or self-exaltation ("exalteth himself"). Seated in the "temple of God" he will imitate or counterfeit God's presence in the Church ("shewing himself that he is God") and demand obeisance and worship. We cannot deny that some of this is already happening (as yet in a limited fashion) in the contemporary Church, for a spirit of rebellion and pride is already at work in many congregations around the world. It is evident that in many of these local assemblies there is little or no respect and submission to the delegated authorities that God Himself has established in His Church.

With increasing frequency false ministries are appearing among God's people, and especially persons that claim to be apostles (Revelation 2:2) and prophets (Matthew 24:11; 2 Peter 2:1) but at the hour of truth prove to be impostors. In many churches certain spurious and strange manifestations are taking place, that have neither biblical precedent or proof. Everywhere you go now, you hear false prophecies, that frequently lead gullible believers astray and away from the path of righteousness and truth.

During the years of His public ministry, Jesus Christ had to cleanse the temple of God in Jerusalem on two separate occasions. At the beginning of his ministry, He found the temple converted into a "house of merchandise" (John 2:16). With a whip in His hand, He "cast out" all the animal vendors and money changers. Sad to say, three years later, the same merchants were back in full force, having transformed the temple into something even worse, a "den of thieves" (Luke 19:45-46). He again had to "cast out" the intruders, proving that by not living in strict obedience to the Word of God, the believer can be re-infested by demons (Galatians 5:1).

This story helps illustrate what Jesus said in Matthew 12:43-45, where He declared that when evil spirits are cast out of a man, they will always seek to return accompanied and reinforced by others even more malevolent than themselves. If they achieve their purpose, the latter condition of this man will be much worse than the former one (2 Peter 2:20). He will again need to repent and submit to a powerful and persistent deliverance prayer. The battle for freedom could take even longer than the first time, for these demons will put up a fierce fight against any efforts on our part to dislodge them.

TEXT #8

"Do ye think that the scripture saith in vain, The spirit that dwelleth in us lusteth to envy?"
—James 4:5—

This portion of Scripture might arouse heated debate, because the translators of some of the more recent versions of the Bible took their liberty in capitalizing the word "spirit," which causes this text to cease referring to a spirit (most certainly a demon) and to instead refer to the Holy Spirit. In the Greek language there are no capital letters. The use of them is a matter of interpretation, that might reflect the preferences or prejudices of the translators.

The word "dwell" in this verse is derived from the Greek verb *katoikeo* that means "to inhabit" or "to establish residence." Therefore, the literal translation of this passage ought to be: "Do you think that the Scripture saith in vain: The spirit that took up residence in us tends towards envy?"

I keenly remember when I was preparing for the ministry during the early '50s, hearing one of my Bible professors state that there is not a single reference to the Holy Spirit in the Book of James. If that be the case, these modern translators made a grievous mistake in capitalizing the word "spirit" in the verse under consideration.

This verse can only be interpreted correctly as you study it in light of its context. The whole passage (that begins in James 3:15 and ends in 4:7) speaks mainly of some of the manifestations of our carnal nature, such as envy, bitterness, strife, greed, lust, friendship with the world, pride, etc. Paul asserts that "this wisdom descendeth not from above, but is earthly, sensual (carnal), devilish." Behind the greed and envy and other works of the flesh, you will usually find demonic spirits in full operation, taking advantage of the occasion to create an atmosphere of strife, confusion and disorder in our personal lives, homes and churches.

Many agree with the second part of James 4:7 that literally says: "Resist the devil, and he will flee from you." Resist is a military term, used also in Ephesians 6:12-13 and 1 Peter 5:8-9, which refer to our constant battle against Satan and his demonic hosts. Our effectiveness in spiritual warfare against the demon spirits that could be operating outside or inside of us depends entirely upon the fulfillment of the condition laid down in the first part of the same verse: "Submit yourselves therefore to God..." To live in constant victory over the enemy, you must submit daily to the will of God, for otherwise the principalities and demons will refuse to submit to you. Your authority over Satan and his dark kingdom depends upon your living in subjection to God and to His delegated authorities both in the church and in the human race at large.

A Final Word

I trust that the analysis of these biblical cases and scriptural texts has convinced you of the fact, that under certain circumstances a born-again Christian can be infested, polluted, oppressed or bound from the inside by demon spirits and, therefore, needs to resolutely seek his deliverance from such evil powers that are attempting to destroy him.

After ministering deliverance for 35 years, I am more convinced than ever before that this experience is for Christians alone and not for unbelievers. The Bible calls deliverance "the children's bread" (Matthew 15:26), and, in truth, only God's children have a right to receive it. It doesn't seem strange, then, that in the model prayer—known in most English-speaking nations as the Lord's Prayer—Jesus advised His disciples to pray asking their Heavenly Father to deliver them from "the evil one" (Luke 11:4, NKJV).

If non-Christians come to us for deliverance, the first thing we do is present them with the plan of salvation, so they can repent, believe and surrender to the Lordship of Jesus Christ. If they refuse to do so, we refrain from praying for their deliverance, for we have discovered by long and sad experience that it will be quite difficult (if not impossible) for them to be set free from bondages and curses, and, if they are, they will immediately lose their freedom, for Satan will claim his legal rights to indwell and possess them since they are still a part of his family and kingdom (Matthew 12:43-45). We would not be doing them a favor by setting them free, for the demons that were cast out will return in full force accompanied by others and their latter condition will be worse than their beginnings.

Before obtaining the deliverance of her daughter that was "grievously vexed with a devil," the Syrophenician woman had to confess Jesus as Lord (Matthew 15:21-28). The Scriptures declare that "whosoever shall call upon the name of the Lord shall be saved" (Romans 10:13) and/or "delivered" (Joel 2:32). It also bears witness that "no man can say that Jesus is the Lord, but by the Holy Ghost" (1 Corinthians 12:3). Evidently, the Holy Spirit was already working in her life for her own benefit and for the well being of her troubled daughter.

The Gadarean demoniac, before his deliverance, cried out in a loud voice: "Jesus, thou Son of the most high God..." (Mark 5:7), fulfilling the condition laid out in John 20:31 and 1 John 4:15 that when you believe and confess that Jesus is the Son of God you receive eternal life. No doubt, the moment he knelt before Jesus in an act of humiliation, surrender and adoration, something marvelous began to take place inside, that prepared him to experience God's liberating and transforming power.

Today, I am fully persuaded that in these last days the Ministry of Deliverance is indispensable for the survival of God's people and for their readiness for the Coming of Christ. He promised to come for a Church both "holy" (Ephesians 5:27) and "unblameable" (1 Thessalonians

92

3:13; 5:23; Jude 24), and though it is quite evident that the Church is not yet ready to meet Him in the air, we can be sure that God is going to do whatever is necessary to prepare us for that glorious event. In Daniel 12:1-2, He has promised to deliver "every one that shall be found written in the book" of life, and this is to take place before the resurrection of the dead. The Deliverance Ministry (that was restored to the Church about 40 years ago) is another step in the renewal and preparation of the Church for His Second Coming.

The Scriptures teach us that everyone that has this "blessed hope"—the hope of His coming (Titus 2:13) and of the resurrection of the dead (Acts 23:6; 24:15; 26:6-8) "purifieth himself, even as he is pure" (1 John 3:3). Our duty as Christians is to "cleanse ourselves from all filthiness of the flesh and spirit, perfecting holiness in the fear of God" (2 Corinthians 7:1). As part of the sanctification process, we need to be delivered from the defilements "of flesh and spirit" that are caused by evil spirits that might be operating somewhere in our being. And the sooner we do it, the better, because we don't know the day or hour of His coming (Mark 13:32). If after examining your personal life you come to the conviction that there is a strong oppression in your life or home caused by demons or curses hurled on you or your family by secret enemies, please don't hesitate to seek out experienced help.

To the pastors and leaders who have been reluctant (and perhaps a little fearful) to get involved in deliverance, I want to encourage you to try your hand at it. Your churches need it desperately. Among those who attend your church there are some who are no doubt seriously affected by evil spirits, ancestral curses, hexes, illnesses of mysterious origin, vicious habits, etc., that can only be helped effectively and permanently by means of this ministry. Counseling and therapy, on the basis of modern psychology, cannot liberate the captives; only Christ, on the basis of His redemptive work on the cross of Calvary, can do so.

The authority to cast out demons is not a special gift received by a few privileged individuals, but is the duty and privilege of all believers. The Lord Jesus included deliverance in the Great Commission when He said: "And these signs shall follow them that believe; In my name shall they cast out devils..." (Mark 16:17). According to verse 20 of the same chapter, in obedience to this command the disciples "went forth, and preached everywhere, the Lord working with them, and confirming the word with signs following." God bore witness to the authenticity of their message "both with signs and wonders, and with divers miracles ... according to his own will" (Hebrews 2:4), deliverance included.

Therefore, my dear brother and sister, rise up in the power of the Holy Spirit and face the enemy squarely, valiantly. Use the authority that God has given you (Luke 10:19) to rebuke, bind and expel Satan and his minions from the places which he has taken by usurpation. Apply the benefits of redemption by faith and you will be surprised when you see what God by His Spirit will do in your life, home, church and community.

Continental Ministry Crusade, Inc.

We would like to commend to you the ministry of Continental Ministry Crusade, a non-denominational faith ministry organization which for more than 50 years has conducted evangelistic crusades, trained qualified pastors and established more than 500 indigenous churches, in order to meet the spiritual needs of suffering humanity.

The author of this book, Rev. Norman Parish, is a respected veteran missionary with more than 40 years of fruitful ministry in Central and South America. He and his wife Betty are based in Guatemala and have labored for Christ in 12 countries of Latin America. He has unselfishly and faithfully served the Lord as a missionary, teacher and evangelist throughout the Americas. In addition he is considered one of the early pioneers of the ministry of deliverance.

We confidently endorse this ministry as worthy of your financial support.

You may contact this ministry or send donations to **Continental Ministry Crusade, Inc.** at their offices:

American Address	Canadian Address
P.O. Box 670	P.O. Box 23503,
Webb City, MO 64870	Willowdale, Ont. M2H 3R9
Fax (417) 781-1696	Fax (416) 492-1162

Any gift will be acknowledged with an official receipt for income tax purposes.
Field Address: Apartado Postal #2 - 01901 Guatemala, C.A.
E-mail: parishcmc@c.net.gt

Impac Christian Books

332 Leffingwell Ave., Suite 101
Kirkwood, MO 63122